CIN 2/07

This book should be returned to any branch of the
Lancashire County Library on or before the date shown

3 1 MAR 2007

2 5 MAY 2007

- 3 MAR 2008

- 3 MAR 2008

8/1/19.

# Bright and Breezy . . . .
# BLACKPOOL

## A Pictorial Journey through Blackpool's Past.
(Including A Short History of The Tower, and Blackpool's Three Piers)

*Catherine Rothwell*

PRINTWISE PUBLICATIONS LIMITED
1991

Published 1991 To mark the Centenary of the laying of the foundation stone of the Blackpool Tower.

Published by
PRINTWISE PUBLICATIONS LTD.
47 Bradshaw Road
Tottington, Bury.

Warehouse & Orders
40-42 Willan Industrial Estate
Vere Street, Salford M5 2GR
Tel: 061-745 9168

ISBN No. 1 872226 13 2.

Edited and additional material by

*liff Hayes*

PRINTED AND BOUND BY
Manchester Free Press, Paragon Mill, Jersey Street, Manchester M4 6FP. Tel: 061-236 8822.

# ACKNOWLEDGEMENTS

The late A.D. Abram; Charles Ashton; the late Vic Baldwin; Abraham Barlow; Blackpool Library; James Burkitt; Stanley Butterworth; Mrs M. Dooley; Fleetwood Chronicle; The Graphic; Mrs E. Hall; The Lady; Lancashire Library; Lancashire Life; Miners' Home; Harold Monks; Red Rose Postcard Club; E.G. Rothwell; Rev.Dr.E.J. Rothwell; Ron Sever; Ralph Smedley; Dorothy Sturzaker; Diana Winterbotham.

DEDICATED TO: MY GREAT GRANDFATHER AND GREAT GREAT GRANDFATHER,
who both loved Blackpool.

# INTRODUCTION

By BBC North's Top Laughter maker, one of Radio Lancashire's top personalities and the man who introduces the BBC's Radio Goes to Town in Blackpool each year. The man they said could make a stick of rock smile... Little N.T.

*Norman Thomas*

Blackpool is brash, bawdy and vulgar but at the same time beautiful and romantic, which is why I love it!

Go anywhere in the world and you'll always find something to write home about, but you can go to Blackpool every year and there is always something new, something exciting, something that draws you like a magnet, some strong aphrodisiac that excites the senses like no other seaside resort in the World.

When I was a lad the family holiday would, in those days, be the usual week of 'day-trips' but the highlight was always the day my Dad booked the charabanc to Blackpool. The excitement started the night before with whispered plans at bedtime, between the brothers three, of all the things we would do, whilst downstairs Mum and Nan were busy making enough sandwiches to feed an army. Come the day we were never disappointed and I still remember that the day was always planned so that we spent time on the beach, we then marvelled at the array of temptations as we walked the Golden Mile, and we'd finish up spending every single penny of pockets money, and more beside, trying to out-brave each other on the Pleasure Beach rides. The journey home was always one of happy oblivion as exhaustion gave way to sleep.

I have returned to Blackpool annually and have stayed in lovely quirky boarding houses anbd also the best hotels, but Blackpool itself is still the same. Every year there are adventures new, and every year it yields yet more surprises. One of the joys of becoming a father is that I can now start to enjoy Blackpool all over again through the eyes of a child, and so we come full circle.

This book will let you wander down memory lane and remind you of the love affair we all have had with Blackpool. It's funny how time plays tricks on the memory, but I can honestly say that the two things I will always remember is that my Blackpool was always full of sunshine and laughter.

Norman Thomas can be heard daily for 2 hours of gentle fun on the following stations:—

# FOREWORD

To visitors in their millions, the Tower, Piers, the Illuminations, the sea and the trams all combine in the magical spell woven by
BLACKPOOL....

Blackpool is everything . . . but something different to each group of visitors. The words of Reg Dixon's (Mr Blackpool) signature tune "Oh I Do Like to Be Beside the Seaside" seem to sum up the resort. BRIGHT.....the Illuminations; and BREEZY....the sea air; FREE it cost nothing to stroll the front and the inImitable Golden Mile; and EASY.....Easy Going: they really do cater for all ages and tastes, and like the visitors to enjoy themselves.

Pleasing everyone has always been Blackpool's number one aim. And in that it has succeeded with style. It is epitomised in the 'wish you were here postcards' - hard-working landladies with hearts of gold and H.P. Sauce on groaning tables; large bosomed, nagging wives; "birds" and red nosed boozers are all fair game for vulgar depiction, but somehow they emerge as hearty and healthy as the tangy sea breezes trying to whip them off the stands.

My father, still visiting Blackpool in the 1950's, his annual pilgrimage to Mecca, gloried in the music of Toni and the North Pier Orchestra. He sat ensconced for fleeting hours like a lord,in the Sun Lounge with a brown paper bag of Victoria plums in his lap. Later, in the same spot, Raymond Wallbank played the organ whilst visitors hired deck chairs to bask in tropical warmth. Outside, serried ranks of deck chairs face the sun at 30p a session for turning brick-red or Benidorm brown as the spirit moved you; or to cool off there were deep-sea fishing competitions from the jetty, gate money a mere 10p before it was storm damaged.

Each summer season, to the rumbustious hundreds of thousands thronging the Golden Mile, clutching candy floss and "Kiss Me Quick" hats in breezes guaranteed to knock any self-respecting cobweb for six, big eyeing Coral Island but making for the Tower and North Pier, all this represents value for money; a looking forward to Autumn and the Blackpool Illuminations.

Year after year unassailable Blackpool girds itself up for the race it has never stopped running. One recent Easter brought conferences attracting 15,000 visitors, the largest being the R.A.F. Association with 4,000 delegates.

All round our coast there are piers in parlous states, but not so in Blackpool. The most famous, The North Pier, stronger than when originally built, alongside the Tower and Winter Gardens remains one of Blackpool's trump cards, in a hand full of aces.

This year 1991 marks the centenary of the laying of the foundation stone of Blackpool Tower. The summer of 1891 saw the start of an ambitious plan to erect an 'Eiffel' Tower in Blackpool, and it is difficult to realise just how ambitious this plan was and how it nearly failed. There were in fact plans for Towers to be built in other seaside resort in Britain but only Blackpool managed it. The full story is told later in the book.

On the 90th Anniversary of its completion in 1984 the present owners 'New Leisure Corporation' gave the Tower a £1.3 million face lift. Included in that was the revamping of the lifts which during the season carry about 7,000 people a day skywards to look down on. . . **'Bright and Breezy BLACKPOOL'.**

Catherine Rothwell

Catherine was born in the Prestwich area of Manchester and has resided on the Fylde Coast of Lancashire for the past thirty years. During her career she has been Deputy Borough Librarian of Fleetwood and after reorganisation in charge of all Local History and Reference for the Lancashire District of Wyre.

Her success in writing has led to appearances on B.B.C. and Granada Television, and Catherine has been interviewed on B.B.C. Radio Lancashire, Radio Piccadilly, Coventry and Warwick. Isle of Man Radio and Red Rose Radio. She enjoys lecturing to the W.E.A. and to local Associations and Groups.

# The Story of Blackpool Tower

The lure of Blackpool, the most famous family seaside resort in the world, is symbolised by its Tower, which has become both trademark and international landmark. Fame spoke for itself many years ago when a postcard addressed simply "The Tower" was endorsed in Palestine, "Try Blackpool, England."

When Gustave Eiffel constructed his famous tower for the Paris Exhibition of 1889, the London-based Standard Contract and Debenture Corporation planned to erect similar towers in seaside resorts throughout Britain, but only Blackpool had the determination and tenacity to achieve one.

Registered on February 19th 1891, The Blackpool Tower Company Ltd., hoped to acquire for £94,000 the full benefits of a contract. For £60,000 the original Aquarium formed by William H. Cocker was to be had alongside the chosen site, but, "failing to carry out their obligations the Standard Company were released by the Tower Company on condition that the purchase price was reduced to £72,800." The Tower Company thus effected a saving of £21,200 and for £4,000 managed to purchase from the Central Promenade Company the animals, birds, fish and tanks. It was a good start but local support was poor when shares were offered, despite the enthusiastic example of Mayor and Alderman John Bickerstaffe. For his northern grit and prescience, routing London capitalists, he was rewarded in 1898 when grateful shareholders presented a four-foot silver model of the Tower, now insured for £60,000 and a focal point in the Memory Lane Exhibition. John also received a massive silver salver in 1912 and was made a Freeman of the Borough for his role in an amazingly successful venture that never looked back.

Local memories recall muscular navvies who dug out the foundations with shovels (no mechanical aids) and on September 25th 1891 the foundation stone was "well and truly laid" by Sir Matthew White-Ridley with mayors and dignitaries watching. There followed a

sumptuous banquet at the Imperial Hydro featuring a lavish display of the council's silver and candelabra and a long menu including grouse, calf's head, haunch of venison and Ice Pudding a la Eiffel.

Messrs Neil and Sons' Contract for Tower Foundations was £3,000; Messrs Heenan and Froude's Contract for the Tower Metal £42,000 exclusive of Lifts; the architects were Maxwell and Tuke; engineer R.J. Read, and with W.Bell and J.J. Wilcox responsible for building the Tower the four legs of which were encased in concrete 35 feet square. The freehold site covered 6,040 square yards.

It was 1894, the year that the Abana was wrecked off Norbreck in a 135 m.p.h. gale that they opened the Tower Circus and other buildings. Whit Monday, May 14th was the great day. The Vault, Pavilion Bar and Cafe Bar followed in the August to refresh the 70,000 that turned up. From the start, a great attraction was the ascent by hydraulic lift, it being a completely new experience. In 1896 the Company made a profit of £30,000 due to the enterprising John Bickerstaffe

*Taken on April 10th 1893 when the metal structure had reached 168 feet. Note the Aquarium and Menagerie which were later incorporated into the main building.*

*The photograph displaying "Blackpool Tower Company: Aquarium Aviary and Menagerie" was taken in 1892 just as the construction at the base was taking shape.*

travelling here, there and everywhere like the Scarlet Pimpernel, advertising country-wide. Soon the Tower overshadowed all other entertainment, quite eclipsing the Gigantic Wheel which opened in 1896, weighing 1,000 tons, designed to impress but alas destined for dismantling in 1928.

Much was made of the Tower's vital statistics and visitors boggled at these alone. Working in duplicate, the lifts travelled from the 55 feet level to the 373 feet level. More than five million bricks were used in the Buildings; the original weight of steel in the Tower alone was 2,493 tons, cast iron 93 tons, the weight of the girders in the Buildings 985 tons of steel and 259 tons of cast iron. The height of the Tower to the top of the Flag Staff is 518 feet, to the Crow's Nest 480 feet, but few people realise that the flag flying on the sixty foot flag-staff can be ripped to shreds within a few hours in a high wind or that this perennial magnet for millions is capable of a one-inch sway at the top during a 70 p.m.h. gale. Very hot weather also produced interesting but catered for expansion of metal.

There was a fire at the top on July 22nd 1897, a

frightening occurrence but no one was hurt although £1,000 worth of damage was done to the Platform, and ascents closed for the season. A 1901 official guide and programme found under old linoleum informs - "The attractions of the 'Palace of Pleasure' include an aquarium, menagerie, monkey house, aviary, bear pits, roof gardens, Old English village, Tower ascents, grand ballroom and grand salon. The pleasure of the Tower can be enjoyed for a nimble sixpence."

In a constant march forward of success, by 1903 the Tower Company had bought the Alhambra with its expensive but hitherto loss-making interior. A grandiloquent gesture was the free opening of the Tower Ballroom to 8,000 people in 1900, celebrating the victory of Pretoria. By 1909 "Matcham's masterpiece", the Grand Theatre, had been added to their assets for £47,000, and complete control of all the best amusements in the town was guaranteed by the subsequent purchase of the Winter Gardens in 1928.

Blackpool was the first in pioneer flying exhibitions, the Tower indispensable with its range of coloured flags signifying "flying in progress" (red), "flying suspended" (black). October 18th 1909 heralded a very wet spell, eliminating two whole days, but in the next year's Aviation Week, French pilot Tetard flew round Blackpool Tower. Watched from the Tower, Graham-White landed on the sands, the first man to transport mail by air. Crowds also watched from Snaefell summit, Isle of Man, as the intrepid aviator flew round the island. Trips round the Tower, now commonplace, were made possible only by such prize-winners as Rougier, Farman and Paulhan. At four o'clock one morning the world's largest airship the R101 encircled the Tower, which she had made her landmark, prior to crossing the Irish Sea under a full moon.

Famous names, not merely those of entertainers, seemed to proliferate in the salty air: Sir Stanley Baldwin and Sir Malcolm Campbell came in 1932; politicians, record-holders, whatever or whoever was "best" sooner or later arrived; Gracie Fields, Tallulah Bankhead, George Formby, Gertrude Lawrence, Anna Neagle, Jack Buchanan, Vesta Tilley, Frank Sinatra, Bob Hope, Paul Robeson, Marlene Dietrich, Ted Heath and his Orchestra, D'Oyley Carte Opera, Gypsy Ivala clairvoyant daughter of world-famous Gypsy Boswell. Joe Loss - King of Rhythm. Down the years issued a glittering kaleidoscope of talent from the world of music, oratory, song and dance and popular entertainment.

Throughout its long history a record of expansion at the Tower has been maintained. Re-decoration, refurbishing, remodelling is never-ending. Twenty trained

**The Foundation Stone:**
*Laid with much ceremony on September 25th 1891 by then Blackpool M.P. Sir Matthew White-Ridley in the presence of the Mayor, Sir John Bickerstaffe. At the time of printing there was still much speculation as to the whereabouts of the container filled with papers and souvenirs of the day. Much searching under and behind the stone during recent work has not uncovered it yet.*

men, riggers, painters, welders, work constantly to preserve the metal which takes 4 tons of red lead and 1½ tons of oxide paint every time it is covered.

The world's greatest ring circus had forty polar bears performing one bank holiday early this century, four Indian elephants and the Schaffers, world-famous acrobats in 1903, for on Whit Monday three years earlier the Circus had been re-opened after a complete remodelling including the stables and dressing rooms. 1933 saw the Circus Table, Ram and Steelwork all renewed, the same year that the Circus entrances were altered. Charlie Cairoli joined in 1939, favourite clown for forty years. The 1981 "circus classrooms" taken by ringmaster Norman Barrett unfolded a history of circus tradition, using stars in full dress costume and equipment.

Unforgettable is the spectacular water finale.

John Bickerstaffe and directors saw the first cinema show in the Tower Ballroom when steamboat "Queen of the North" flickered for a few magic minutes. In the twenties the first big cinema picture "Hindle Wakes" was shown. People fought to get in, but a revolution in cinema entertainment has since taken place.

Whit Mondays have been traditional days for opening innovations at the Tower, e.g. Chinatown, later renamed Oriental Village, and Old China Tea Houses. The Whitsun of 1914 featured Promenade Tea Rooms and the opening of an underground passage between the Tower and Palace Buildings, originally Alhambra. Another year it was the Roof Gardens with rockery later developed into a free-flight aviary, adding more attractions. Here was sited the Midget Town inhabited by human midgets. This became Tiny Town and Side Shows in 1933 following the Indian Village, Oriental Bar and the installation of new passenger lifts.

But the Tower Ballroom is especially world-famous. In May 1899 the Tower Company re-opened the Old Pavilion, redesigned by Frank Matcham into a gorgeous, gilded, Renaissance affair. Under the proscenium's bold motto "Bid me discourse I will enchant thine ear" lilted the music of Mr Oliver Gaggs and his Orchestra. One grand popular ball in aid of the Lifeboat Band was held on December 5th 1909 with dance programmes shaped

like fans. For thirty years Reginal Dixon, "Mr Blackpool", played the Wurlitzer organ, becoming an institution with his signature tune "I Do Like to be Beside the Seaside". Phil Kelsall and Arnold Loxam are today's red-coated players of this mighty organ which, like most Tower 'props' has an interesting story. A three-year overhaul by organ specialists J.W. Walker of Suffolk begun in the winter of 1977 cost £50,000. With its 150 stops made to Reginald Dixon's specifications it is the greatest instrument of its kind in Europe, coming originally from Illinois.

At the outbreak of the First World War Clara Butt had electrified a patriotic audience by her stentorian rendering of "Land of Hope and Glory" at a time when the Ballroom was given over to the making of silk parachutes. The wars disrupted pleasure at the Tower, but entertainment mingled with serious business, helped to ease the strain. The Victory Ball 1918 featured more northern grit when war-wounded from Squire's Gate Convalescent Camp, angry at their non-inclusion, clamoured to be let in amongst the silks and taffeta and starched shirts. After the first world war

Storm at Blackpool

*'Walk Over The Waves' was one way of advertising the new North Pier. The sea has always been one of the fascinations for the visitor even to sending postcards showing how bad the weather could be. As in this 1920's postcard.*

£100,000 was spent to offset the deterioration of ironwork.

During the second W.W. all sorts of flag-wagging speeches were given in the Tower and the tones of a variety of people from Lady Randolph Churchill to Horatio Bottomly rang out to moral or money-raising rallies . The Chief of Police used the Tower for viewing early blackout conditions from the top and declared "This won't do." Top of the Tower had literally been 'Top Secret'· with 90,000 servicemen billeted in Blackpool and the Tower's appearance strangely altered by radar antennae. Such a landmark for the enemy prompted a Fleetwood councillor to demand its pulling down (after all Fleetwood's Grain Elevator had to go). But usefulness and sentiment won the day. 1946 saw 80,000 people pass once again through the turnstiles.

Just before the Christmas of 1956 a solitary cigarette led to appalling destruction in the Tower Ballroom. Surely the saddest day in its history. Fire-fighters worked like mad to prevent the inferno reaching the metal legs, which could have melted with disastrous conse-

quences. Their concrete emplacement, wisely thought out in the foundation laying, prevented this, but the Ballroom's gorgeous interior was ruined. Craftsmen came out of retirement to re-paint 2,000 feet of ceiling murals. Forty tons of scaffolding provided platforms for gilders, artists and plasterers who between them used 1,000 gallons of paint and 6,750 books of gold leaf. Recreating the ornate splendour of this world-famous Ballroom took eighteen months and cost five million pounds. It was with pride and joy that it was re-opened on May 23rd 1958, exactly as it appeared in 1899. Another generation gazed at the amazing rococo, the golden tiered boxes, Italianesque scrolls, chandeliers, cherubs and drapes, all for their delight. Soon afterwards the Tower Company sold the splendid Palace Ballroom together with theatre and annexe for demolition, making way for Lewis's Store. Strange to say, all that dancing started in the nineteenth century in the open air when most participants wore clogs. Another

departure was from the old original aquarium with its 16,000 gallons of water. In 1960 the Orchestrion Organ known as the 'Grand Old Lady' of the Tower left Blackpool for a Birmingham Museum. The menagerie animals were found new quarters and the zoo converted. Tower Children's Ballet also came to an end after sixty years.

1961 announced a "big face-lift" planned for the Tower, consisting of a completely new promenade front for the seventy year old building to cost more than the whole original outlay. A new 240 foot frontage designed by MacKeith Dickinson and Partners used reinforced glass fibre, illuminated pillars in opal glass, and armour-plated glass. Wisely, Victorian panels, ceramics and art -deco interior is preserved, the Tower having been declared a listed building on October 10th 1973.

"The Tower is sold in 16 million pounds takeover," announced the Evening Gazette on October 31st 1980. Thorn E.M.I., owners since 1967, offered the Tower,

Winter Gardens and Golden Mile Amusement Centre to Trusthouse Forte. A rival bid of a consortium of Blackpool businessman tried to keep the Tower in local hands but Lord Bernard Delfont won. However, only three months later, it was announced, "Tower goes up for sale again." Two years later on January 15th 1983 the Tower and Winter Gardens complex and all three piers were bought by First Leisure Corporation for 37?8F? million pounds, thus becoming Britain's biggest independent leisure company and gaining a huge slice of Blackpool's entertainment comparable with Las Vegas U.S.A. Even John Bickerstaffe who was never afraid to spend would have been surprised. This escalation necessitated each Pier having its own Manager, the Circus continues, although no animals are now involved and the planned improvements to the ring have been deferred a year. General management of the Tower has been passed to Mr. Stephen Brailey.

Biographers of Blackpool Tower must find themselves constantly stuck for superlatives. The raising of popular entertainment standards, coupled with the health-giving prop-erties of sea-side living and facilities second to none, created a conference town whose population doubled in twenty years. No resort has enjoyed greater popularity, and the centre of its attraction, a monument to its enterprise, is the beloved "red pepper-shaker", that tapering intricacy of girders which is always the centre of Blackpool life. THE TOWER.

During the Queen's Jubilee its top was painted silver. Strobe lights flash at the top of the Tower where a million passengers are carried each year in its modernised lifts. Lasers, marvels of modern technology, figure in the greatest free show on earth, "The Lights". Les Dawson summed it up when he switched on the lights in 1986; "The greatest tourist magnet in the Western Hemisphere"; Red Rum said nothing when he did the job. But when all is said and done, after a hundred years, John's original recipe for success remains the same.

*A rare postcard, one of the few showing the magnificent Indian Pavilion (the white dome to the right, at the end of the pier).*

# The Piers

"Blackpool is lucky in the possession of a couple of splendid piers." Abel Heywood's Penny Guide to Blackpool and Fleetwood reported in 1880. In the end, of course, there were three piers and inevitably some confusion of names but the following should explain:

## THE NORTH PIER

On June 27th 1862, on the occasion of the first pile of the North Pier being screwed into the clay, Major Francis Preston, Chairman of the North Pier Company, prophesied it would grow into "One of the Most Amazing aggregations of Public Amusement in the World".

On May 21st of the following year, he formally opened the 1,405 feet-long 27 feet-wide structure into which had gone 12,000 tons of metal, a structure claimed to be the finest "marine parade" in Europe. Its original cost was £20,000 but to this was added a fur-

ther £30,000 as ideas developed. Built from designs by E. Birch, Civil Engineer, it proved an elegant addition to the attractions of Blackpool.

For this red-letter holiday Blackpudlians insisted on bringing back the Town Crier, relegated by "progress" as an anachronism, out of step with the march of time. His stentorian roars couched in record-breaking decibels greeted tippers spilling out of the Lancashire & Yorkshire Railway trains which had been chuffing in from all directions, some since dawn. Fun-loving spirit overflowed; so did the pubs. Flags and bunting galore fluttered in the salty air whilst daredevils threatened to dive off the end of the pier at the first moment presented; some did. Incidentally, aquatics became a speciality of the North Pier, its waters deciding some of the principal championship events in the swimming world. Major Preston's twelve-pounder cannon, the only piece of artillery Blackpool could boast, vied with the Town Crier. For a town constantly on the up and up all this marked the advent of a new era of enterprise. a town whose only problem was accommodating its population explosion. But where there was a will, there was a way. Six in a bed and working shift systems, or sharing horses' hay to lie down on after a day in the breezes, who cared as long as they had arrived in Blackpool?

Supported by several brass bands, a grand procession of Freemasons, Friendly Societies, fishermen, bathing machine attendants, lifeboat-men, dignitaries and the multitude proclaimed to the country "this substantial and safe means for visitors to walk over the sea". The gala opening was considered worthy of a front-page engraving in the Illustrated London News. Within three

years they added a jetty for pleasure steamers the "Queen of the Bay" and the "Clifton" providing trips and cruises for thousands, from the end of the Pier. But the restless, ambitious Directors craved even more limelight, using fabulous personalities to promote their ways.

From the Pier Head flights of steps descended to the iron extension where passengers could land from the steamers at any state of the tide, thus putting Blackpool in direct communication with the Lake District, Isle of Man, Llandudno, Southport and Liverpool. Aquatic sports also were held from the pier extension. The extension made the pier 1,650 feet long.

In 1874 they increased the area by another 5,000 square yards to give the Pier its greatest glory. The Indian Pavilion was built on the north wing of the Pier Head. On the south wing of the pier shops, refreshment rooms and a bandstand eventually appeared.

Totally authentic, The Indian Pavilion was designed from studies of Hindu palaces and temples, principally the Temple of Binderaband. Results were sufficiently

CENOTAPH AND NORTH PIER, BLACKPOOL.

spell-binding to hit news headlines in such tributes as ''strongest and most beautiful pier in Europe''. Certainly this spirit of enterprise made North Pier without rival in the country.

Nightly concerts were given in the Pavilion which was capable of holding 2,000 people. In the golden years before fire destroyed the Indian Pavilion some of the greatest instrumental and vocal artistes performed before Blackpool audiences: Sir Charles and Lady Hallé; Sims Reeves; Madam Patti; Signor Foli; Madame Trebelli; Mr Charles Tree; Mr D. Ffrangcon Davies and countless other celebrities, now a study in nostalgia. The North Pier's reputation for high-class orchestral music was established by Edward de Jong, possibly the most eminent flautist of his day. Masterly batons brought North Pier concerts into the favourable notice of the best critics who spread the glad news through the national press. Professor Simon Speelman, linked with the Manchester's Hallé Orchestra as an eminent viola player, further increased its fame. When it was destroyed by fire on September 11th 1921 the salvage was sold for £310. It was rebuilt in 1925, but again destroyed by fire on June 19th 1938.

The little theatre or arcade was built at the landward end of the pier in 1903 and this lasted until 1965 when it was dismantled. The pierhead bar and cafe was replaced in 1937.

That distinguished beauty, the Duchess of Argyll, Princess Louise, drew more crowds when she opened the widened Promenade. North Pier's entrance was set back, harmonising with and enlarging the Square where people congregated. An arcade of shops in an onion-domed pavilion made for further enhancement when walking over the waves without danger of sea-sickness.

Catastrophes too have pulled in the crowds to the North Pier. A large Norwegian barque, ''Sirene'' helpless in the grip of a storm, smashed against the south side of the entrance, sweeping away six shops. The crew scrambled up ropes and girders onto the pier planking, one occasion when there was no need for the lifeboat to put to sea. Next day, for news travelled fast, crowds scrambled for sodden furs and costume jewellery strewn on the sands by the tide. Even more spectacular was the foundering of the 'Foudroyant' Lord Nelson's flagship in June 1897, a wooden sailing ship anchored for exhibition purposes. Unaware of what the Irish Sea could wreak with its sudden summer storms, the Captain was astonished to find his ship wrecked off the North Pier, pounded by waves 60 feet high. Drifting heavy oak timbers did hefty damage and again crowds poured in, my father amongst them, to collect souvenirs. All sorts of objects were made from the oak and copper of this incomparable vessel. They sold like hot cakes, so much so that not all could have been genuine or the ship would have had to be four times larger.

When the pier first opened twopence was charged for entry, then reduced to one penny. Various tolls were charged until in July 1981 the toll was dropped altogether. In the January gales of 1968 40 feet of the jetty was damaged, but quickly repaired in response to public demand. The North Pier is now a listed building.

ROUGH SEA OFF NORTH PARADE, BLACKPOOL.

*A dramatic postcard from 1905.*

One of the first postcards to refer to Central Pier, printed at the turn of the century.

CENTRAL PIER, BLACKPOOL.

# CENTRAL PIER

It was the immense popularity of the North Pier that inspired the building of this Pier originally called South Pier. Major Francis Preston formed the South Blackpool Jetty Company, six of its eleven directors being also on the North Pier Board. Built under the supervision of Colonel John Mawson, the first pile was driven on July 3rd 1867 and the Pier opened in haste on May 30th 1868, in readiness for the season.

The decking was 1,118 feet long by 24 feet wide, supplemented by an iron jetty extending a further 400 feet into the sea. The principal engineer was Benjamin Sykes and the contractors Messrs R. Laidlow and Sons of Glasgow. The original capital of the Company was £10,000 but almost immediately it was increased to £20,000 and on September 29th 1873 to £41,000 for the purpose of purchasing steamers.

Although it was not an immediate success, Robert Bickerstaffe the man appointed Manager was full of ideas. He organised a steam boat trip to Southport at 1/- per head, dropping Pier charges. With a German Band playing for dancing the Pier became famous for its all day open air dancing which started as early as

5.30 in the morning and went on continuously until 10 at night. Advertised as the "People's Pier" it aimed to please the working classes, but Summer Shows were not started until after World War II.

Various alterations were made to the original structure including a new iron jetty at the end and an extension of the Pierhead to give more space for dancing, with a toll-house resembling a Chinese pagoda. It proved to be one of the most popular areas in all Blackpool for open-air dancing, screened from the wind by a framework of wood and glass. In the 1880's admission for dancing was only one halfpenny.

Swimming and diving displays have featured in its history and regular steamboat crossings to Liverpool, Barrow and Llandudno, Lytham and Morecambe. Cross-channel races were organised in the 1890's between Central and North Piers. In 1909 a roller skating rink was opened on the Pier which proved to be a great attraction. Even as late as 1962 a new improved 170 feet long wind screen was erected round the ever popular dance area.

Storm damage in 1964 caused the jetty to be shortened and the Pier has suffered three fires in its 120 year life, but compared with North Pier's damage Central Pier got off lightly. In 1976 the jetty at the end of the Pier was demolished by dynamite. The Dixieland Palace which was completed in only ten weeks at a cost of £150,000, was opened in 1968. When fire swept the Dixieland Bar in 1973, 1,500 people had to be evacuated. Central Pier's Amusement Arcade is known as the Golden Goose.

*The rebuilt North Shore, showing its "wonderful Promenades".*

*A very early photograph of Central Pier just after its opening, referred to as 'South Pier' at this time.*

# SOUTH PIER

In March 1893, this was the third pier to be opened. South Pier or Victoria Pier came about through demands from South Shore residents for a music and social centre rivalling North Pier. When the South Pier Jetty Company was floated, £50,000 was quickly subscribed. The Pier was erected by J. Butler and Company of the Leeds Stanningley Ironworks. Iron was used for the piles and steel for the decking.

In March 1893 it was complete except for the Grand

Pavilion designed by J.D. Harker. This eventually would hold an audience of 3,000 people. Although the pier was only 429 feet long, it was wide enough to accommodate 36 shops, a band stand and shelters.

The entrance to the pier was set back in 1902 when the promenade was widened and in 1918 the Victoria Cinema de Luxe was opened. Some twenty years later the pier entrance was altered again, and the pier itself widened by 20 feet. Also at this time a Regal Pavilion was provided which was capable of holding 1,300 people. For additional strength reinforced concrete piles were driven 40 feet into the sand beneath the Pavilion. This work was undertaken by H.H. Vickers and Son.

Two big fires, the first in February 1958, the second in the same month of 1964 destroyed the Grand Pavilion and the Rainbow Theatre respectively. Rebuilding in time for the Summer Season in 1964 led to a new theatre being constructed in just eleven weeks. Lanes Amusements Ltd., were controlling the Pier in 1963 but by 1968 Trust House Forte took over. Freddie and the Dreamers, Hylda Baker, Tom O'Connor, Morecambe and Wise and many more, too numerousto mention, show biz personalities have all appeared.

By 1905 the great Promenade undertaking between Victoria Pier and North Pier was complete.

*A lovely postcard of the new South Pier in 1893. Note that it is referred to as Victoria Pier.*

SOUTH SHORE BLACKPOOL

*To lead people to the newly opened Victoria or South Pier the front between the North and South was widened, and made attractive for the crowds to stroll down from pier to pier. This postcard dates from 1906.*

# BRIGHT and BREEZY BLACKPOOL
## A Pictorial History

Apart from William Hutton and his daughter Catherine who enjoyed visiting and writing about Blackpool in the 18th century, travelling all the way from Birmingham, this man, Rev.William Thornber, was the earliest chronicler of the town. His family lived in Breck Street. Poulton-le-Fylde, where his father was a local magistrate. It was his mother's great interest in old furniture that kindled his interest in local history, so that eventually, between church duties, he wrote his History of Blackpool in 1837. It is still a good read although purists have called some information unreliable.

As priest in charge of St. John's, Blackpool, he resided at the vicarage situated where the Winter Gardens now stand. To gather information he talked to old inhabitants and walked miles over the mosses in all directions, ranging as far as Rossall. The town and port of Fleetwood had not yet been built. Born in 1803, William was interest in the ancient church of Bispham, where he was married by the brother of the Lord of the Manor, the Rev. Charles Hesketh.

CARLTON TERRACE NORTH SHORE BLACKPOOL

*Rock and Company, well known London Engravers, were commisioned in 1867 to prepare plates for Blackpool, the seaside resort bidding fair to outstrip Brighton in popularity. Victorian shawls, bonnets, crinolines, horse-drawn landaus and carriages are evidence of the more genteel aspect which took over in the the Autumn and Winter when the crowds of trippers from the mill towns had returned home. The prints of Carlton Terrace North Shore; Regent's Terrace and Brighton Parade, part of Blackpool's sea front are dated November 1867.*

Rock & Co., London.                                      Nov. 9, 1867

REGENT'S TERRACE AND BRIGHTON PARADE BLACKPOOL

25

*This photograph shows Hoo Hill Windmill, one of the many in ancient Amounderness, later known as the Fylde. The mill was struck by lightning in July 1881. Blackpool air had long been renowed for prolonging life. Born about 1737, Mr W.Bonny of Hoo Hill, known by William Thornber, could walk from Blackpool to Preston and back on the same day even when he was 80, and lived until he was 91. In spite of their age, Jemina Wilkinson, 104, and her neighbour Mrs Banks 99, still helped with the harvest.*

*Whinneys Heys, Blackpool, shown in this rural scene, was the site of the present Victoria Hospital. The name originated from the name of the yellow gorse (Whineis) which surrounded the house that James Massey of Carleton built in Elizabeth I's reign. The Veale family lived there until the 18th century it was one of the calling places of Thomas Tyldesley) then like Burn Hall it was let off in parts to farming tenants. For a number of years it survived as part of the Nurses' home for the hospital.*

*To make way for the growing town many farms had to go, but as land values rose, some farmers were not unwilling to part with property. Old Bonney's Farm became the site of the King Edward Hotel; Old Revoe Farm the Branch Library and Gymnasium. At Hound Hill in 1860 a tiny family grocer's shop run by Mr J. Parker, and his wife and daughters became the site of Bannister's Bazaar, now the wide-spread Hounds Hill Centre.*

This photograph shows early days before there was much building along the cliffs. The carting away of sand and gravel by such horses and carts as seen here had to be stopped as rough seas eroded the cliffs at an alarming rate.

The grant of the Borough's Commision of the Peace is dated August 27th 1898 and given under the hand of Queen Victoria. The first meeting of the Town Council in the new Town Hall was held on January 4th 1898 when Joseph Heap was Mayor, the first Mayor of Blackpool having been Dr. W.H. Cocker.

A man on horseback, cobbled areas and no motor traffic indicate that this view of Talbot Square with the Church of the Sacred Heart on the left dates back to the early 1880's. Claremont Park Terrace and Princess Parade had already been constructed. Crowds were drawn to Raikes Hall Gardens, Hornby Road, to view "Niagara", a simulation of the great falls. The grand main entrance of stone with raised letters "Raikes Hall Park Gardens and Aquarium" was takem down in 1904. Dancing and entertainments were offered at Belle Vue Gardens in 1886.

*The lonely nature of the Sand Hills at South Shore is shown in this photograph from 1889. The Star Inn provided tea and coffee and also the sale of Dublin stout for people who came out for the day from Blackburn, Preston, Bolton and Manchester. One attraction was the Gipsy Encampment at South Shore. Here were found tents and gaily coloured caravans, some of which were still around in 1905 when the Pleasure Beach was coming into being.*

Sarah Boswell was the famous "Gipsy Sarah" who could read fortunes. Many visitors turned to her, "crossing her palm with silver" for a look into their futures. In this postcard issued by Burns and Ashton of the old Victoria Pier, Sarah aged 99, is shown with her grand-daughter standing beside her on Blackpool sands. The gift of sooth-saying and second-sight was supposedly passed down from generation to generation in the Gipsy tribe.

In this picture of Bank Hey Street from c. 1875, where on the left the present Lewis's is built, many shops present a quiet aspect. On the corner can be seen a notice, "To the Fire Brigade Station". The pointed spire of the Infant Classroom, erected in Bank Hey Street in 1856, is out of sight, but the useful corner shop and the top-hatted driver with his hansom cab in the deserted street are signs of the times. Further up on the right is Victoria House quite an emporium. The long barber's pole next to the shop window draped with sacking belongs to Mr. Stirzaker, "Haircutter and Perfumer". On the corner of Sefton Street and Bank Hey Street at number 38 was Holt's, Ladies' and Children's Outfitters, of Bank Hey House.

*Talbot Square in 1870, the days of the Theatre Royal. The Square has known many joyful gatherings including Royal visits. Old photographs show it seething with thousands of people at the Coronation Festivities of King Edward V11 on June 26th. All the buildings were surmounted by flags, bunting and loyal addresses: "God Save the King. Long Live the King." What were perhaps the forerunners of Blackpool Illuminations also figured in Talbot Square on that occasion, showing E.R., a crown and festoons of coloured lights. The large building on the corner, once the Theatre Royal, Free Libary and Reading Room, had by then become a Wine Lodge. Immediately before that it was Talbot Dining Rooms when the building had no verandah.*

FREE PUBLIC LIBRARY.

**BLACKPOOL FREE PUBLIC LIBRARY AND READING ROOM.**

Opened by the Earl of Derby, K.G., 18th June, 1880.

*OPEN DAILY, from 9 a.m. to 10 p.m.*

*This shows Mr Harland's impression of the Blackpool Free Public Library and Reading Room which was opened by the Earl of Derby on June 18th 1880, in those days "open daily from 9 a.m. to 10.0.m." In the 70's this building was the Theatre Royal. In 1896, before the Carnegie building in Queen Street served the community, the Old Free Library was in Market Street. On the ground floor was the Paragon Hosier and General Draper, Gentlemen's Outfitters and Specialists in Umbrellas. Drummonds, the Tobacconists, were next door.*

*In Blackpool's Jubliee Year 1926, the Chief Librarian was Rowland Hill, but the first librarian to be appointed was Hannah Eteson. In 1880 the first Free Public Library was opened by Lord Derby K.G., with 1,600 books housed in the Octagon Room in the building on Talbot Road that later became Yates's Wine Lodge.*

*By 1890 Hannah Eteson's assistant, Kate Lewtas, had become Librarian.*

33

This engraving of Foxhall, Blackpool South, shows one of the few interesting old buildings in the area. Preserved in early years as the Foxhall Hotel or Vauxhall, it dated back to Charles 11's reign when Edward Tyldesley built it in hopes of reward after being staunchly loyal to the Royalists. Around the property he flung a high wall made from cobbles brought from the beach. The diarist Thomas Tyldesley lived there for a time. The origin of the name may be a tethered fox, which was kept at the gate. A large kitchen garden, apairy, ancient fig tree and a number of priest holes were features of this Hall which was at one time involved in an annual race meeting held at Layton Hawes.

Bathing vans in 1865 bore the names of proprietors J. Wylie, W. Salthouse, R. Ormond, W. Singleton, R. Swarbrick and W. Cragg. Beached high and dry on the gravel, as in this serene photograph, were small pleasure boats; The Victory; Gentle Annie; Civility; Faith; Mary Jane; Charity; Leader. The two-masted Faith belonged to Edward Banks. Jack Stanhope, a local character, lived in one of the fishermen's whitewashed cottages which were then immediately above the beach, facing the sea.

John Wylie's cottage, for generations home of the Wylie family, was not far away. James Wylie, shoemaker, Daniel Atherton, merchant tailor of Vine Cottage, John Ingham, boot and shoe maker; Miss Simpson, confectioner; and Mr Coulson, draper, were all there to serve both residents and visitors. Frequent trips by horse and cart were made to Poulton-le-Fylde for extra requirements, especially on "flesh days" when meat and fish were purchased.

Commissioned to photograph the Front at Blackpool in 1865, Mr J. Mudd of St, Ann's Square, Manchester, set up his camera at low water at what was to become the head of South Pier. In the previous year the first North Pier had been opened. The promoters of the Blackpool South Jetty Company decided that a second pier was necessary and submitted a scheme to Parliament. To make their case Mr Mudd was to photograph the Front from the Star Inn at the South to Claremont Park cliffs on the North. In those days ten to twelve feet of gravel protected the Front. At South Beach shingle was high enough to allow pleasure boats and fishing boats to lie high and dry for most parts of the year but by 1883 the foreshore was denuded of this protection.

In the year of Mr Mudd's historical panoramic photograph the Local Board obtained powers through Parliament to borrow £30,000 to make a Promendade and extend the hulking.

South Beach from Central Pier is shown in 1880.

WINTER GARDENS, BLACKPOOL.

*The Crystal Palace, Alpine Hall and Uncle Tom's Cabin were amongst the earliest efforts to amuse people when the sands, beach and pier had given all the fresh air treatment the visitors wanted. On Whitegate Drive, Belle Vue Strawberry Gardens did well, but it was a carriage drive away. Bigger gardens at Raikes Hall took over but as soon as the Winter Gardens came into being in a position near to the promenade the other two faded away. Dr. W.H. Cocker, who impoverished himself with his enterprise in the entertainment world, was the driving force behind the Winter Gardens, a pleasure dome ahead of its time, shown in this photograph of 1890. He further experimented by building his aquarium and menagerie on the Tower site.*

The 1882 poster of the Prince of Wales Baths gives much information; "Blackpool is famous for its baths but of these, the Prince of Wales on the promenade are the largest and best, having cost £15,400." Other superlatives were added in that year: "the finest in the United Kingdom." White tiles covered the floor of the great plunge, 107 feet long and 83 feet wide. Massive pillars of granite "rose out of the water to support the balconies." The 120,000 gallons of water needed was pumped from the sea into tanks where it was filtered and purified. 61 dressing rooms, supplied with towels, brushes, combs and suitable costumes surrounded the baths. Turkish, Russian and Vapour baths could be indulged in and visitors were able to watch some of the finest swimmers in the world.

Of many visiting bands, choirs, glee-singers and troupes to Blackpool this band of Sappers of the 28th Company Royal Engineers, 1894, made its own instruments. In the 1970's came Texans with their Horses. The list of the truly famous who have performed in Blackpool is endless. The town could attract world famed artistes like Caruso, Nellie Melba and Lilly Langtrey, the darling of Edward V11 who built a love nest for her in Bournemouth; Vesta Tilley, destined to become the wife of Lord de Freece; Stan Laurel and Oliver Hardy; George Formby Senior and Junior; Tom Mix; George Robey; Harry Lauder, Spectacular productions such as Savage South Africa involved performing elephants, and genuine Transvaal Boers. The arrival of the Mail Coach, the original Gwelo coach attacked by Matabele tribesmen in 1896, had the very driver on that occasion James Keighry, taking part. Prince Lobengula the famous Matabele Chief, was on view daily, admission threepence. In presenting the spectacular, Blackpool was unrivalled in the whole country.

*Development of Dr. Cocker's Zoo and Aquarium to the present Tower was guided by John Bickerstaffe. The phenomenal growth of the town, largely a result of the Tower opening, also helped the Winter Gardens to keep going. With a third Pier, the Pleasure Beach and the Palace for amusements, Blackpool burgeoned into the "Wonderland of the World". This marvellous scene from 1895 shows Central Promenade with its well built houses, equipped with long gardens. - Landaus, horse buses, long-gowned ladies in the favourite black bombazine of the period - even a small boy busy with a wheel barrow. Over all the "Eiffel" Tower looms supreme.*

*Fifty years ago the Curator at Blackpool Tower Zoo commented that Blackpool butchers must not supply ewe-mutton to feed the lions. "These lions are pretty temperamental about chages in food," he said, which led to a poem in the Blackpool Times based on Albert and the Lion made famous by Stanley Holloway.*

# LION'S SHARE

*As Albert were passing by t'Tower,*
*he heard a most horrible noise.*
*T'lions were cutting up proper*
*And t'keepers were losing their poise.*
*They were gazing at King of Beasts dumbly,*
*Bewildered, downcast and perplexed.*
*When "What's to do?" Albert asked humbly,*
*They answered, "Them lions is reight vexed.*
*We offered them ewe-mutton broth for*
*Hors-d'oeuvres to the four o'clock feed,*
*When they roard in carnivorous wrath for*
*An injunction to stop the cruel deed.*
*We fear we have set up a trauma -*
*They're highly strung beasts, not just mard;*
*The unhappy occurrence will form a*
*Reminder to be on our guard.*
*When lions are clemmed, you must study*
*The likes and dislikes of the den,*
*Not fret their psychoses with ruddy*
*Ewe-mutton fit only for men."*

Indian Lounge, Winter Gardens, Blackpool.

19. Park Rd - Thanks for card which I duly
received. We did not get home until last
Tuesday but the previous Tuesday I commen-
ced with a severe cold, had to call in the
doctor, & he kept me in bed for a week, &c

The magnificent range of buildings in the Winter Gardens included the Indian Lounge, "ornamental illuminated gardens and promenades, a veritable Fairyland" in which the visitor could spend all day after paying sixpence or move on to the "most magnificent Palace of Amusements in the world", under the same roof. Grand Concerts in the Floral Hall were held every afternoon from 1 p.m. to 3.30 p.m. in December of 1899. Marches, waltzes, polkas, "galops", and a selection of popular songs were played. The General Manager of the Winter Gardens in those days was J.R. Huddlestone. On Christmas Day at Her Majesty's Opera House the Messiah was performed with full orchestra and chorus of 300 in this the "most comfortable and elegant theatre in Great Britain, lighted with electricity throughout".

"Compare the advantages you get here," said Mr Huddlestone, "to those offered elsewhere. All persons who visit this superb theatre have the privilege of free admission to the Winter Gardens." No other theatre in the country could match that.

*The ornamental fountain in Talbot Square, a good meeting place for local worthies, was erected ten years before this busy scene in the 1890's. From here horse buses, wagonettes, landaus picked up passengers. The horse bus in the photograph is bound for the Oxford Pleasure Gardens on the route. On the right of the fountain, out of the picture, was the shop owned by J.S. Todd, a silk merchant who also sold greatcoats or Ulsters. J. Wright, confectioner, was next door. However, all these buildings were demolished to make way for the Town Hall. From the fountain could then be seen the old Union Baptist Chapel in Clifton Street, which was pulled down to make room for the General Post Office.*

*For the crew of the wrecked Sirene in 1892, as for that of the Huntcliff which grounded in the St. Anne's sandhills, this was a happy landing. The vessel came hard up against the North Pier, allowing the crew to climb up ropes onto the decking, although the pier itself was badly damaged by the collision. This was two years befor the wrecking of the Abana and one year before the opening of Victoria, South Pier. On every such occasion crowds came in by train, hoping to salvage something from the wreck and its cargo. People had to be warned against taking sides of bacon from one wreck, but soldiers from the garrison town of Fleetwood took no heed and roasted the meat on spits over blazing fires lit from driftwood on the sandhills.*

THE NEW AMERICAN IRON STEAMSHIP "CHAMPION." OF THE VANDERBILT LINE

Reproduced from "Harper's Weekly"
By permission of Harper & Brothers

*Soon after leaving Liverpool in August 1848 the emigrant ship Ocean Monarch was lost at sea in a raging inferno which could be seen from Blackpool. Many jumped overboard and dead bodies were washed up along the Fylde coast as far as Lytham, where an entire Irish family was buried. The Austria suffered the same fate. This American iron steamship, Champion, from those years, one of the Venderbilt line used for transatlantic crossings, was also seen off Blackpool in its regular journeys.*

In the early hours of December 22nd, 1894 the timber ship 'Abana' grounded in a great gale off Little Bispham. The previous day it had snowed and it was so cold that the spray froze on the beach. When the Abana was wrecked, the Blackpool lifeboat had to be taken to Bispham and launched from the sandhills in a 135 p.m.h. gale. This is the ship's bell which was presented to Robert Hindle of the Cleveleys Hotel for his part in the rescue, including sending a boy on horseback to alert the lifeboat. All 16 crew members were saved, and even the captain's dog. The Abana was built in New Brunswick, Canada in 1874 and it's remains can still be seen in the sand.

Mr. and Mrs. Hindle eventually presented the bell to St. Andrew's Church where it is now rung at every service of interment in the Garden of Remembrance.

The first Blackpool lifeboat, the 'Robert William,' was launched in 1864. In September 1885 a large crowd gathered in Blackpool to see the four local lifeboats drawn up with cork-jacketed crews alongside. The 'Robert William' the 'Charles Biggs' of Lytham, the 'Laura Janet' of St. Anne's and the 'Samuel Fletcher' of Manchester were then launched together to the cheers of the onlookers. The following year saw the 'Mexico' disaster when the St. Anne's' lifeboat crew and all but two of Southport's crewe were drowned. This disaster, the worst in R.N.L.I. history rocked the country.

Amongst the changes that took place under the Blackpool Improvement Act of 1899 was the abolition of the Toll House in Clarmont Park and the Toll Gate near The Gynn. This would be the scene on Blackpool's beach at that time. R. Penswick's bathing vans, complete with their advert for Jones Sewing Machines are still in use and drawn up ready to trundle into the sea. Some visitors sit under large black umbrellas, protecting themselves from the sun. The cliffs, still crumbling, can be seen in the middle distance, site of The Old Camera Obscura.

In 1887 a battle of Flowers was held when the Mayor and Mayoress, Alderman James and Mrs. Fish, were escorted from their house in Dean Street in a landau covered with blooms, a spectacle which drew many visitors.

Two stages in the construction of the Big Wheel which opened on August 22nd, 1896 in the expectation that it would be as successful as the Tower. This was not to be, but it did stand for 30 years alongside the Tower as symbols of the great seaside resort that Blackpool had become. They were both outstanding landmarks. The axle weighing 30 tons, had to rest on 8 columns set in 9 feet of concrete. Rising 220 feet and affording stunning views across the Fylde and the Irish Sea. The whole structure weighed over 1,000 tons.

At first the crowds flocked. Each of the 30 carriages could hold 30 people, but the novelty waned and the carriages lay idle. The Winter Gardens Company decided on demolition and on October 29th 1928 the carriages were auctioned. Some became hen houses, perhaps the ''last of the Mohicans'' remains as the 'Big Wheel Cafe', at Over-Wyre.

47

By way of extra entertainment, the trippers heard shouts from the booths and stalls along the Golden Mile. "Short of cash? Sell your old false teeth." The best female remedies were "Lady's Best Friend" i.e. Mayfield Lill's Female Medicine 4/6d or Dean's Female Mixture at 2/9d. For "weak men suffering from the effects of youthful errors" the answer was Wilkinson's Special Elixir. The truly desperate could book 'steerage passage at low rates, including outfit free of charge on the White Star Line Royal Mail Steamers 'Germanic' or 'Majestic' from Liverpool to New York.

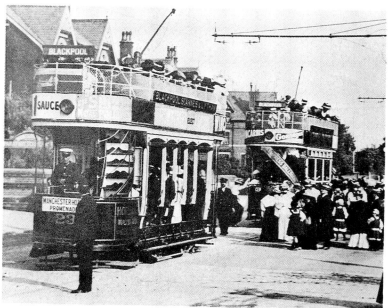

The placing in position of the first rail of the Blackpool Corporation Tramway was on March 12th 1885. The system was operated by underground conduit. As might be expected, Blackpool had the country's first electric trams. They started with 10 cars which could each carry over 35 people, but the great bugbear was 'blowing sand' which often slowed down the system. In 1892 the Corporation took over, and overhead power installed six years later, solving the clogging by sand, but high tides and wind in the roughest of weather can still bring the service to a halt. Two trams from 1900 with their advertisements for 'Shinio Metal Polish' and 'Wincarnis Wine' are just two of the many advertisements the trams were showing at the turn of the century.

*This 1895 photograph shows North Pier and on the right the Tower, which had been opened the previous year. From the 1,850 foot long pierhead, flights of steps descended to the iron extension where passengers landed from steamers at any state of the tide. Under Trinity House regulations the lamp at the end of the pier had to be lit between sunset and sunrise. Besides links with the Lake District, Isle of Man, Liverpool, Southport, and Llandudno, in those days steamers and sailing boats plied continuously to the South Pier, the property of the Jetty Company Ltd. Dancing, an institution in Blackpool, was very popular on the South Pier. Dancers paid one halfpenny at "at a toll house of Chinese architecture" to pass into the space for dancing which was screened from the wind by a framework of wood and glass.*

"I am sorry the dances are over at the Charity Schools..... I have been at Blackpool centre all day." This postcard of rural Bispham is one of the "Fylde Series" and was posted in March 1909. Even then, the old world village atmosphere was appreciated, as so much in Blackpool was being swept away. This is the old Bethel Chapel, built in 1834, which would have been seen by visitors travelling by tram. Most of them called at the Ivy Cottage Tea Rooms, home of the Tinckler family in the 17th century. Many thatched cottages could still be viewed, sketched and painted, but by the 1960's not a sign of antiquity remained.

Mr and Mrs John Ferguson are photographed at their Golden Wedding celebrations. They had been married at St. Paul's Church, Marton, in 1868 and with Mr Ferguson's experience gained in establishing Cherry Tree Gardens, a favourite tourist venue, they worked together on the Marton Nurseries, Whitegate Drive. John was also a Governor of the Baines Endowed School, Marton, one of the three Charity Schools started by James Baines, prosperous woollen chapman. The other two schools were situated at Thornton and Poulton. Replacing an earlier school built in 1838, a new Baines Endowed School was erected 1897.

One of a popular series in the 1920's, this postcard also served as a Christmas card. It may have come from a landlady as they often kept in touch with visitors during the year. Catering and "putting up" people was very hard work, the family having to crowd together in order that every room could be let throughout the season.

The charge for a double bed in the early 1900's was 2/- a night, and 3/- for two beds if children also had to be accommodated. One penny was charged for potatoes and one penny for milk, visitors usually buying the rest of the food - bread, bacon, eggs, meat and paying the landlady for cooking it. Some landladies added "a charge for the cruet". A cheap family holiday resulted but there was friction in some houses when visitors suspected inferior meat or fish had been substituted. On the whole Blackpool was always known for giving good value.

On October 2nd 1926 the Earl of Derby officially opened the Marine Promenade and Stanley Park. Colonnades, sunken gardens, rock gardens, a waterway and cliff rockery, were features of the Promenade. It was an extension of that completed in 1905. Some 80,000 tons of gravel, all obtained from the site, and 9.000 tons of cement were used in the construction of the Sea Wall, which at its base was 14 feet thick. Old tram rails were driven into the sand, 8 feet apart, as king piles, to give strength.

Stanley Park was designed and constructed under the supervision of Messrs Thomas Henry Mawson, Landscape Architects of Lancaster. The whole scheme cost £250.000. Motor launches 'Lady de Freece' and 'Lady Parkinson' were presented by Sir Walter de Freece and Sir Lindsay Parkinson respectively for use on the large Park Lake.

51

*This solemn occasion is the laying of the Foundation Stone for Blackpool's new Police Courts in 1892. James Cardwell, who was three times Mayor, is flanked by top-hatted Commissioners, Town Clerks and other dignitaries. He is wearing the ermine robes and ceremonial chain of office. Blackpool's Charter of Incorporation as a Municipal Borough, by command of Her Majesty Queen Victoria, is dated January 21st 1876. The Grant of Borough Arms by Heralds' College was another important parchment (June 10th 1899) in the town's history.*

"Portraits taken and processed whilst you wait" can be seen alongside an advertisement for the Tower in this happy holiday scene at Uncle Tom's Cabin in the early 1900's. A photographer is in evidence, setting up his tripod in the open foreground, whilst on the roof are the wooden figures which helped to give the Cabin its name. It was an attempt to link three carved Negroes with Harriet Beecher Stowe's book "Uncle Tom's Cabin". Actually Tom was Tom Parkinson, husband of Margaret who started it up with a Sunday refreshment stall, a day when visitors were in plenty. She sold ginger bread and ginger beer.

The forerunner of this building was a small, wooden hut of which Robert Hardman Taylor and his wife became owners in 1858, also running a lodging house in what became Abingdon Street, Blackpool. Uncle Tom's developed into a centre for entertainment, a fiddler playing for dancing on the greensward. On this site the Reverend William Thornber saw the beautiful Rose of Rossall, when even then it was popular for dancing in the open air.

Just one of the many theatrical celebrities that visited Blackpool, Ellaline Terriss and her baby in the early 1900's, can be seen on this postcard issued by Rotary Photgraphic Plate. For three nights only in March 1900 Charles Wyndham and Miss Mary Moore appeared in a performance of Rostand's play, Cyrano de Bergerac. "For this grand production over 100 persons will be seen on stage at one time." The play was shown at the Grand Theatre and Opera House, Manager T. Sergenson. The theatre acclaimed as Frank Matcham's masterpiece, the prettiest theatre in the Kingdom. Wilson Barrett, Henry Beerbohm Tree and Edward Terry all sang its praises as the best-appointed and most artistic, transcending even those of London.

Great Marton Windmill, adjoining the Oxford Hotel, one of many near Blackpool, was demolished in 1902, as shown on this postcard. A smock mill, constructed of bricks, it was five storeys high. Like that at Staining, a few miles from Blackpool; the cap could be turned into the wind by a wheel and rope. Thomas Moore, a Marton miller, was interested in developing South Shore in the early 19th century. Census returns for Marton village show that William Salthouse was inn keeper at the Clifton Arms. The mill was then inhabited by Nancy and John Whalley. Thomas Moore was the village wheelright and Richard Houghton the blacksmith. The smithy and wheelwright's shop were always adjacent as here, and were later converted into a garage. Across Wheel Lane was Cuckstool Field where the ducking stool for suspected witches was once situated.

54

*Perhaps Blackpool's greatest seaside spectacular, a free show, was the wrecking of Lord Nelson's flagship the 'Foudroyant'. In her day one of the most famous ships in the world, it was strange that the country's number one playground by the sea should be the scene of her end.*

*Anchored three miles off North and Central Piers, for two weeks she was an object of interest to thousands of holidaymakers. Steamers daily conveyed people "to tread the decks and explore the Admiral's cabin" of this historic vessel which had twice been a refuge for Royal families and had made under Lord Nelson the memorable chase of the Genereux. "Crowd on every stitch of canvas and make the Foudroyant fly to the capture," roared Nelson on that occasion. But with an inexperienced crew Foudroyant met her doom in June 1897 in a sudden storm. Dismasted and floundering helplessly, she finally grounded near the Hotel Metrople. All her crew and the owner, Wheatley Cobb, were saved by the Blackpool lifeboat. Mr Cobb, staying at the Wellington Hotel, employed a salvage company, but before Foudroyant had had the last word, two further vessels were lost trying to retrieve her wonderful oak timbers.*

*Another good view of the cliffs at North Shore and of an early uncluttered beach in 1900. "Having splended weather. Hope you are better for your holiday". Wrote May on the back of this postcard. Along these golden sands the Lord of the Manor, Peter Hesketh, once enjoyed six miles and more of sand-yachting. In the 1830's he brought back from his house Maison Dieu at Dover, a "new-fangled" sand yacht which he kept at Rossall Hall. It was not surprising that he thought it a good idea to build a seaside resort and port at Fleetwood, with such a natural playground on his doorstep.*

MAXIMS FLYING MACHINE

SOUTH SHORE BLACKPOOL

On August 10th 1904 the year Blackpool became a County Borough, this postcard was sent from Blackpool to the Isle of Man. "I have seen Albert carrying a stone bottle on the end of a cane," reads the message, no doubt referring to one of the resort's magnetic attractions that season. A large notice in the centre announces "Site for Hiram Maxim's Captive Flying Machines." the place is South Shore where Blackpool's Pleasure Beach has since spread into a large complex.

To some, this postcard may be a somewhat amusing reminder of 4 o'clock one November morning in 1925 when the giant airship R 101, the world's largest, circled around the Tower prior to crossing the Irish Sea. It was a wonderfully clear night with a full moon, specially chosen for the test flight, and my brothers were bundled out of bed to see it. Blackpool's built-in tradition was always to deal in the superlative.

"We are having a nice time. By jove it is full here today." This from Rose, in Aviation Week, October 1909 when aces H. Farman, M. Paulhan, M. Leblanc, H. Latham, M. Fournier performed in an Antoinetter Monoplane, a Farman Biplane, a Bleriot Monoplane and a Wright Biplane. Although the weather was rainy and windy for this unique occasion, the crowds flocked in their thousands. From the Blackpool Gasworks Mr Spencer climbed to a height of 1,000 feet in an airship 70 foot long.

The photograph taken in Blackpool's first Aviation Week shows a Voisin Biplane. On May 24th 1919 - A.V. Roe introduced a daily air service which flew passengers from the beach, South Shore, to Southport and Manchester. All such events, including Sir Alan Cobham's Air Circus, were recorded on postcards.

*A lady visitor with her pet dog, photographed at the Studio of A.C. Fox, Layton Avenue, near the Laundry. In the early 1920's his charges were a shilling a dozen for postcards, sixpence for half a dozen postcards. It was popular to be photogaphed with pet, biycycle, tennis raquet, cricket bat, or dresssed for work e.g. miners, postmen, delivery boy. Still a novelty, photography boomed at Blackpool. There was so much scope and alongside grew the interest in collecting postcards. Families filled album after album and asked friends to send a card whenever they went away. Surely. the origin of the holiday phrase "Wish you were here!"*

Amongst this group of pleasure steamboats is the 'Great Britain', a name skittishly applied because the huge leviathan of that name was then in the national news. The jetty at the end of North Pier was where people embarked for trips as far away as North Wales. The 'Bickerstaffe' and the Morecambe Steamboat Company's 'Roses' may be amongst the group. In old photographs the 'Bickerstaffe' who had a number of stormy passages, is often seen grossly overloaded with trippers. Trips to Llandudno, Barrow, Liverpool and even Douglas, Isle of Man were available for the sporty Edwardians.

Two Royal visits are shown here. The first being that of H.R.H. Princess Marie Louise when she came to open Princess Parade on May 2nd 1912. Amidst huge crowds her landau is seen leaving the Lancashire and Yorkshire Railway, Talbot Road Station. The Sand Express, headed by engine "Annie", brought sand for the New Promenade and pile driving went on throughout 1911. When the Promenade and Sea Defence works were opened in 1905 a sand pump was used to pump 165 tons of sand an hour into the cavity behind the sea wall.

In a crowd of ex-service men with the Mayor and Lord Derby beside him, the young Prince of Wales, later Duke of Windsor, is shown on a visit to Blackpool in June 1927. the month when a total eclipse of the sun brought 100,000 spectators to view it.

In his 1927 visit, the Prince of Wales opened the Miners' Home at Blackpool. This is one of many photographs taken on that occasion, showing the staff of nurses, cooks, cleaners, laundry girls etc. It was then called the "Lancashire and Cheshire Mineworkers' Convalescent Home", where sick miners could recuperate in the health-giving Blackpool air. As requirements for the miners have changed, so has the name of the home to the "Lancashire and North Staffordshire Miners' Convalescent Home" and the "Lancashire Paraplegic Mineworkers' Holiday Unit". Sir Jimmy Saville attended the 60th Anniversary. A Home Improvements Scheme was completed in 1976 but the 90's have revealed attempts to sell off part of this huge magnificently appointed building.

*A Blackpool wedding in the early 1920's. The bride in satin and wearing pearls, carries the most popular flower for weddings of the era, a large sheaf of Arum or Easter lillies. The young man, a stone mason, carved all the names on the War Memorial at Thornton, Four Lane Ends, of local men who had fallen in the Great War. Blackpool was a favourite choice for honeymoon couples, but Mr Justice Rigby Swift, at Manchester Assize Courts, dealing with divorce cases in March 1926, was frowned upon when he quipped, with double edge: "I hear Blackpool mentioned in this court more than any other place in Lancashire. I suppose it is because of the wonderful sea air."*

*A charabanc outing setting off from the Clifton Arms Inn in the 1920's. The children are from Little Marton School. At the front in a bowler hat is Abraham Braithwaite who lived at Mill Lane Farm across the road. It is thought that the Marton innkeeper Thomas Altham who had spent 50 years at the Clifton Arms was the oldest man in the Fylde when he died in 1927 at the age of 81. His parents remembered the earthquake of August 20th 1835 which shook buildings in Lancaster, Kendal, Garstang, Poulton, Carleton, Blackpool and Thornton. Another Marton worthy was Richard Braithwaite of Spen farmhouse. He earned a reputation for making cream cheese, which he packed in small containers made from rushes gathered near Marton Mere.*

76283 J.V.

*The drinking fountain whose foundation stone was laid by W.H. Cocker in 1870 was surmounted by a weather vane and faced the North Pier, one of Blackpool's greatest attractions. The postcard shows the busy scene in front of the pier in 1903 when many improvements had been carried out. It was considered "one of the wonders of the North of England for beauty of design and lightness of construction", but in 1921 a fire devasted the North Pier, destroying the Indian Pavilion. Sadly the elegant drinking fountain had to make way for progess and was removed in 1926. Built across from the fountain, the new Town Hall originally had a spire. The Victoria (South Pier) had been opened in 1893.*

The Tower & Wheel from North Pier, Blackpool. A 34.

*During Lancashire Wakes Weeks this postcard was sent out in thousands, the gigantic Wheel. The "magnetic" tower and rough seas seemingly epitomising the resort. Attractions along the Golden Mile included the Rector of Stiffkey in a barrel, Ubangi Savages, the world's greatest freaks, Tussaud's Waxworks, Epstein's gigantic statue "Adam" and many others which raised hackles and sparked off controversy. But they achieved their objective in drawing crowds to the quaint, vulgar and bizarre.*

*The range of postcards sold to visitors included charming Mabel Lucie Attwell drawings, local events such as the plane that crashed in Swainson Street in 1935, Lifeboatman Fish's funeral, red-nosed, hen-pecked husbands, busty ladies in striped bathing costumes, natural sea scenes such as this, but on nearly all, the Tower figured. One-upmanship was to manage a trip to the top and get a postcard franked "posted from top of Blackpool Tower 518 feet high".*

A replica of the ancient Market Cross, Stocks and Whipping Post from the nearby Poulton-le-Fylde is pulled by a horse in procession at Blackpool c. 1930. Just look at the crowds standing on the roof of the tram and in the Dreadnought bound for the depot! Amongst advertisements which seemed to figure upon buildings and hoardings all over Blackpool are shown here: Bryant & May's Swan Vestas, the Smoker's Match; Catterall & Swarbrick's Sarsparilla and Lemonade at a Soda Fountain. This postcard was issued by R.V. Baldwin, travelling photographer of Poulton. On the beach, "While U Wait" photographs of trippers could be had within minutes. They were printed on small sheets of thin metal.

*Henry Hall, leader of the B.B.C. Dance Orchestra, finds his feet in 1928 at the Blackpool Icedrome with some help from accomplished skaters. n 1841. Henry is one of many celebrities to perform in Blackpool.*

*North Promenade in the early 1960's is seen most unusally covered with snow. The ornamental cliffs were built to retain soil and earth at Blackpool's highest point. The Cliffs, North Shore, are shown in an 1880's guide as crumbling into the sea, some areas already left with only their boulder clay bases. The guide refers to the year 1869 when a January storm washed away 350 yards of the sea fence and carriage drive with 16,000 cubic yards of embankment. On February 28th of the same year a second storm added further to the damage by washing away another 250 yards of sea fence and promenade. It was obviously imperative to incur much expense and labour to make the cliffs safe.*

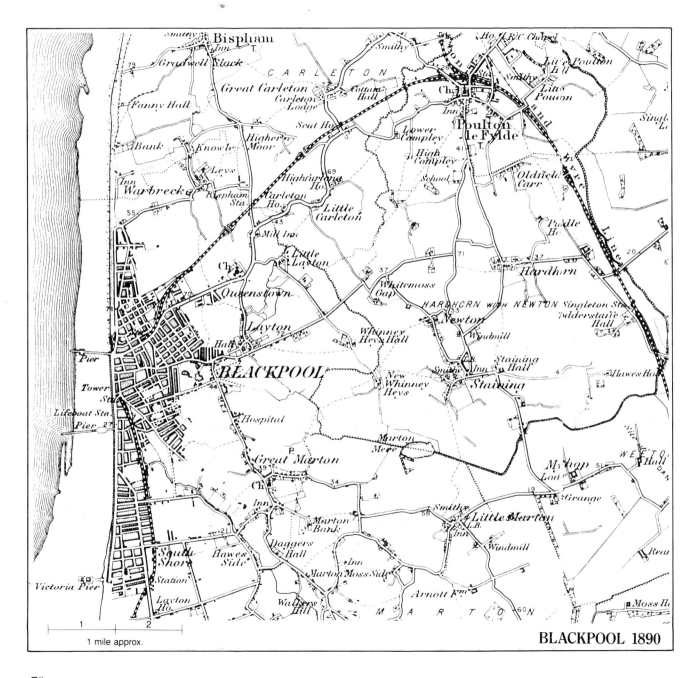

BLACKPOOL 1890

1 mile approx.

OTHER BOOKS TO LOOK OUT FOR BY

# PRINTWISE PUBLICATIONS LIMITED

Illustrations relating to the history of Manchester, Salford and Surrounding District
ISBN 1 872226 00 0   £2.99

Ralston's Views of the Ancient Buildings of Manchester (1850)
ISBN 0 904848-06 X   £2.99

Pictures of Olde Liverpool. A very high quality re-print of a 1927 book.
ISBN 1 872226 02 7   £2.50

Manchester in Early Postcards (Eric Krieger). A pictorial reminiscence.
ISBN 1 872226 04 3   £2.50

Lancashire Halls (Margaret G. Chapman) Sketches, photographs and a short history
ISBN 1 872226 03 5   £3.99

Cheshire 150 Years Ago (F. Graham). Unique collection of 100 prints of the whole of Cheshire in early 1800.
ISBN 1 872226 07 8   Special Price £4.95

Lancashire 150 Years Ago. Over 150 prints reflecting early 19th century Lancashire.
ISBN 1 872226 09 4   £4.95

Ports of the North West (Catherine Rothwell) A pictorial study of the region's maritime heritage
ISBN 1 872226 17 5   £3.95

Southport in Focus. Glimpses of the town's past (Catherine Rothwell)
ISBN 1 872226 15 9   £2.50

Oldham Between the Wars. A collection of photographs from the camera of Edward and Edward Holgate Fletcher. (Edward Perry and Eric Krieger)
ISBN 1 872226 12 4   £2.95

Sunrise to Sunset
(life story of Mary Bertenshaw)
ISBN 1 872226 18 3